DIY

Credit Repair

Beginners' Guide to Credit Repair

Proven method to improve credit rating with credit repair tips and help in understanding credit reports, credit utilization ratio and credit scores

550-649 650-749

-549 750+

Credit Score

Kendyl Jameson

The End
Result

ISBN: 978-0-9992498-3-3

Cover art by Kendyl Jameson.

Visit KendylJameson.com and download the free credit repair workbook.

Paperback also available in Spanish: DIY Reparación de Crédito: Guía del principiante para la reparación del crédito, ISBN 978-0-9992498-1-9.

All trademarks are acknowledged as belonging to their respective companies.

Publisher's Cataloging-in-Publication Data

Names: Jameson, Kendyl, author.
Title: DIY credit repair : beginners' guide to credit repair / Kendyl Jameson.
Description: Delray Beach, FL: The End Result, 2018.
Identifiers: ISBN 978-0-9992498-3-3
Subjects: LCSH Consumer credit--United States--Handbooks, manuals, etc. | Finance, Personal--United States--Handbooks, manuals, etc. | Credit ratings--United States. | Credit bureaus--United States. | Consumer protection--Law and legislation--United States. | BISAC BUSINESS & ECONOMICS / Personal Finance / Money Management
Classification: LCC HG3756.U54 .J363 2018 | DDC 332.7/43--dc23

Other books by Kendyl Jameson

Scan the QR code next to each title to access the book's full description and details online. When the QR code is scanned, your device will open the relevant title on Amazon.

The Pirates of My Soul:
A Transformational Voyage to Self-Empowerment

DIY Credit Builder:
Beginners' Guide to Building Credit

DIY Reparación de Crédito:
Guía del principiante para la reparación del crédito

CONTENTS

INTRODUCTION   1

WHERE TO BEGIN   3

UNDERSTANDING CREDIT REPORTS   7
     Are Credit Reports Fair?
     Prepare Before Borrowing Money

REPORTED ACCOUNTS   12
     Why Do Account Status & Details Matter?

BUDGETING   18
     Why Should I Budget?
     Needs Vs. Wants
     Which Accounts Require Top Priority?

CONTACTING CREDITORS   25
     Contacting Creditors: Not So Scary
     How To Reduce Interest

CONSOLIDATING DEBT   29
     How Do I Consolidate Debt?
     Research & Review Options
     Low Interest Rate Balance Transfer
     How Does A Balance Transfer Work?
     What Are My Savings?
     Balance Transfer Fee
     How Do I Protect Myself If Using A Balance Transfer?
     Which Option(s) Apply To Me?

PAYMENT PLANS   39
     Setting Up A Structured Payment Plan
     Talking With Creditors
     Negotiating & Interest Rates
     Organize Account Details

MAKING PAYMENTS   43
    Strategies For Timely Payments
    Creating Solutions In Payment Emergency
    Seize Opportunities

COLLECTION AGENCIES   48
    Know Your Rights
    How To Resolve The Debt
    What If The Debt Is Not Mine?

APPLYING FOR NEW CREDIT   52
    Should I Apply For New Credit?
    Prescreened & Preapproved Offers

CREDIT SCORE   56
    How Important Is My Credit Score?
    Variables & Credit Utilization Ratio
    Closing An Account

CREDIT THREATS   61
    Possible Credit Threats
    Mail Or Online Fraud & Phishing
    Skimming & Shimming
    Unauthorized Charges

CONCLUSION   68

ACKNOWLEDGMENT   71

ABOUT THE AUTHOR   73

INTRODUCTION

For anyone and everyone wrestling with poor credit or simply wanting to improve their credit rating, this DIY credit repair book will take the mystery out of the numbers.

Easy to read and understand, it walks through the process of repairing your credit to increase your credit score while simultaneously rebuilding your credit trustworthiness. The information provided can be used in whatever order suits your needs, however, it is categorized for easier application.

This beginners' guide to credit repair is written from my experience. There was a time when my financial situation was so bleak, everyone told me to file bankruptcy and get on with life.

But that solution did not suit me. It was the easy way out and like all quick fixes, it was sure to come with a price I did not want to pay.

I purchased my first home and three months later, I was permanently laid off. Although I was not financially irresponsible, I quickly found myself in the middle of a predicament, just like so many other unsuspecting individuals.

Unable to find viable employment due to the economic downturn, I fell behind in everything.

Determined to salvage what I could of my financial status, I chose to fix my credit. Knowing it would take time doing it myself, I believed repairing my credit personally would be better than the mandatory seven-year penalty I would receive from a bankruptcy.

I do not have any regrets with my decision, despite the effort required. In addition, I successfully repaired my credit while learning how to use it—and when.

The entire experience was rewarding and has proven useful time and again. The knowledge gained has withstood the test of time, as well as economic disturbances and recessions.

Numerous individuals have shown an interest in what I have learned and applied. It is for all like-minded people that I have written this guide, hoping it helps others find their way to financial stability. Of course, as times change, new tools and resources become available, and this is only a beginner's guide to credit repair.

Credit is a vast and varied topic. It is impossible to cover everything in a small book and everyone's credit situation is different. Therefore, please be prepared to research in depth any areas addressed within, if questions remain.

The purpose of this book is to get you started on the right foot, going in the right direction. I have included everything in here that I used to fully repair my credit.

On that note, this guide provides *my* proven approach that will not only teach you how to repair your credit, but will also allow you to understand credit reports and the importance of a healthy credit score.

If you choose to personally rebuild your credit, the following process will also provide the basis of how to maintain a desirable credit rating for potential creditors.

Although there are no guarantees of progress or time frames, if you are willing to invest time and effort in your future financial stability, this experience will be well worth the effort.

With dedication, patience and determination, you too can find your credit score reaching for the sky!

Chapter 1

WHERE TO BEGIN

The best way to begin this potentially overwhelming task is to break it down into manageable steps.

When the pieces are in place, it will be much easier to see what you are working with and stick to a plan. The process is broken down into three main steps with examples and explanations to keep it simple.

Step One

✓ *Order your credit report*

Step Two

✓ *Acknowledge expenses and create budget*

Step Three

✓ *Review credit, understand credit report and get started (see following chapter)*

To eliminate some frustration, I suggest reading through the book first, before taking action. Topics will overlap and different options are considered. Before proceeding with any of them, it will be important to know which ones are best suited to your situation.

This is a quick read and explains what you will need before diving in. That said, let's get this project underway!

S*tep* O*ne*

In order to know what you have to do to repair your credit, you must first find out what creditors see when they look at your payment history. This is revealed on your credit report. This is a key factor used to determine if they will lend you money and if so, how much for how long, and at what interest rate.

If you have not already, now is the time to order your credit report. You can order your free annual credit report (credit file) from any or all of the three credit bureaus (Equifax®, Experian®, TransUnion®) once a year.

I like to order mine at different times throughout the year. It allows a sneak peek more than just once a year, ordering from a different one every four months.

However you choose to do it, at the time of this writing, you can start at annualcreditreport.com and order online for instant access, via phone (allow up to two weeks for delivery), or in writing.

If choosing the latter, please visit the website and follow the instructions provided.

Once you have your current credit report in hand, then you can create your strategy.

Step Two

In the meantime, figure out your current monthly and annual expenses. You can make a simple list or create a spreadsheet, depending on your preferred method of organization, *(see example (a) on the following page)*.

In addition to recording the expenses, you will also need to include your monthly income (after taxes), in order to determine how much you have to work with.

Be honest, and if anything, over-estimate on credit cards and other varying expense accounts for a better picture. The following example is conservative and, as you can see, expenses add up quickly.

However, don't become overwhelmed or worry about the numbers and whether or not they line up to keep you in the black. This will come with time.

The goal right now is simply to get it all in front of you to see the reality of what is available and what is needed.

Example (a): Hypothetical Expense and Income Table

Expense	Monthly Amt	Annual Amt	Annual Total
Mortgage/Rent	$500		$6,000
Home Insurance		$1,000	$1,000
Property Tax		$500	$500
Auto Loan	$300		$3,600
Auto Insurance	$200		$2,400
Health Insurance	$200		$2,400
Groceries	$400		$4,800
Electric	$80		$960
Cable/Internet	$100		$1,200
Phone	$80		$960
Credit Card	$400		$4,800
Department Card	$150		$1,800
Gas/Fuel	$150		$1,800
Entertainment	$350		$4,200
Miscellaneous	$200		$2,400
Month Total	**-$3,110**	**Annual Total**	**-$38,820**
Income (after taxes)	**$3,000**		**$36,000**
Difference	**-$110**		**-$2,820**

For this example, the assumption is that certain expenses could be paid for with either a debit card or cash. If not, then those would be factored in through each respective credit card, although you might choose to part them out for the sake of visually itemizing your budget.

In addition, the credit card monthly amount could be represented by the total amount due or the minimum monthly amount requested. However you set it up, be consistent.

Also note that if you are only using minimums due, you should include a column for total debt to that credit card to maintain a visual reality of the total amount owed. Minimums can be severely misleading by the time interest charges are added in to the total, as revealed in chapter 4.

Chapter 2

UNDERSTANDING CREDIT REPORTS

*A*re Credit Reports Fair?

Whether it seems fair or not, lenders always start with the current credit score and a thorough review of the credit report when considering extending credit to a client. An exception to this practice could occur when a client has personal history with a potential lender, but this is not a guarantee.

This process is important to keep in mind, whether you are working to rebuild your credit or planning to ask for a loan of any size.

*P*repare Before Borrowing Money

The best way to approach borrowing money is to know beforehand what lenders will find in your credit history—and if there are obstacles you will need to overcome. This information can help you prepare your credit for a more positive outcome where opportunities exist.

If you start the process at least three months before you apply for any credit, you can address potential hang-ups prior to requesting the loan or line of credit. The minimum of three months is suggested because most items reported on your credit file are ninety days behind. If you want to make improvements that will be recognized, you need to allow for this delay in posting.

If you realize you need more time to make the proper credit corrections and can afford to wait, then postpone applying for the new loan or line of credit until the time is right.

This foresight and preparation could pave the way for a path of less resistance when you complete your application.

If you are not familiar with credit reports and how to read them, now is the time to break that trend. Your financial footprints creating your payment history are recorded on your credit report and speak volumes about your level of financial responsibility.

This information works for you at times and against you at others. As explained previously, although I have been financially responsible, there was a time when my credit file would suggest otherwise.

Obtaining and understanding my credit report proved instrumental in comprehending the importance of fixing and maintaining my credit.

Now it is your turn.

*S*tep *T*hree

With your credit report in hand, review all information for accuracy, including your name, address and social security number.

Review all addresses listed, past and current, and confirm they are places you have lived. Confirm past employment is accurate. In addition, notice any negative information reported to your account.

Depending on what it is, there might be time limitations as to how long the information can remain on your report.

Generally speaking, if the negative information is correct, anticipate seeing it on your file for at least seven years, this includes late payments.

Here are a few common possible negatives to look for, and unless the governing statute of limitations reads otherwise, their time frames generally allowed (always confirm specifics for your situation, including student loans):

» Bankruptcy Filings, 10 years from date of filing
» Chapter 13 Bankruptcy, 7 years from date of filing
» Civil Suits, Civil Judgments, Arrest Records, 7 years
» Collection or Charged Off Accounts, 7 years*
» Foreclosure, 7 years
» Paid Tax Lien, 7 years from date paid off
» Unpaid Tax Lien, Indefinite (must be paid!)

For these specific types of accounts, note the seven year period begins six months from when you fell behind in payments.

Review all accounts and confirm they are yours. In addition, look for suspicious activity that could indicate fraud or identity theft.

Any inaccuracies must be reported to the credit agency that issued the report as well as to the creditor who provided the information. This should be completed in writing and as instructed within the credit report on how to dispute issues.

If the accounts are yours, then confirm the balances and statuses are accurate. Note that accounts may be as much as ninety days behind in reporting payments and take that into consideration when reviewing balances. Confirm payments are being posted correctly, including the amounts paid and payment timeliness.

Identify which accounts report to the credit bureaus and which ones do not. This can be helpful when planning your strategy. Review each account and understand any codes or descriptions as applied, *(see example (b) on the following page).*

Example (b): Example Credit File Labels and Account Descriptions

Account Column Title Descriptions:	
Acct Number:	The Account Number Reported by Credit Grantor
Date Acct Opened:	The Date that the Credit Grantor Opened the Account
High Credit:	The Highest Amount Charged
Credit Limit:	The Highest Amount Permitted
Terms Duration:	The Number of Installments or Payments
Terms Frequency:	The Scheduled Time Between Payments
Months Reviewed:	The Number of Months Reviewed
Activity Designator:	The Most Recent Account Activity
Creditor Class:	The Type of Company Reporting the Account
Date Rptd:	Date of Last Reported Update
Balance Amt:	The Total Amount Owed as of the Date Reported
Status:	Condition of Account When Last Updated by Creditor
Amt Past Due:	The Amount Past Due as of the Date Reported
Date of Last Payment:	The Date of Last Payment
Actual Pay Amt:	The Actual Amount of Last Payment
Sched Pay Amt:	The Requested Amount of Last Payment
Date of 1st Delinquency:	The Date of 1st Delinquency
Date of Last Activity:	The Date of the Last Account Activity
Date Maj Delq Rptd:	The Date the 1st Major Delinquency was Reported
Charge Off Amt:	The Amount Charged Off by Creditor
Deferred Pay Date:	The 1st Payment Due Date for Deferred Loans
Balloon Pay Amt:	The Amount of Final (Balloon) Payment
Balloon Pay Date:	The Date of Final (Balloon) Payment

Account History Status Code Descriptions:		
1: 30–59 Days Past Due	5: 150–179 Days Past Due	J: Voluntary Surrender
2: 60–89 Days Past Due	6: 180 or More Days Past Due	K: Repossession
3: 90–119 Days Past Due	G: Collection Account	L: Charge Off
4: 120–149 Days Past Due	H: Foreclosure	

SUMMARY:
UNDERSTANDING CREDIT REPORTS

Make note of these things when considering your credit report:

» Order free credit report from each credit agency once a year

» Review all information and confirm correct

» Ensure all accounts reported are yours and being reported accurately

» Address any mistakes or disputes immediately and in writing with both the creditor and the reporting company

Chapter 3

Reported Accounts

The posted activity of the reported accounts on your credit report is the guts and the glory substantiating your payment history.

This area requires careful scrutiny.

Review each of the accounts and their status. As previously mentioned, first, make sure they are all yours. If not, then follow the credit agency's instructions within the report to file a dispute or report fraudulent activity.

If there are open accounts that you have closed, then you should notify the credit agency in writing. Provide the account information and the date it was closed.

Any open accounts that were supposed to be closed should be updated on your report. You will have to send written notification to the creditor and request that they notify the bureau. In addition, if you requested to close the account, then this detail should be indicated on your report as well.

When *you* have chosen to close the account, include this in your letter to both the creditor as well as the credit agency.

*W*hy *Do Account Status & Details Matter?*

That's a great question. To many it would seem irrelevant. To creditors, it indicates more than just your borrowing interests and habits.

First: Pertaining to closed accounts, if the account was closed by the consumer, then it is a choice you have made. An example where you might close a line of credit could be a department store card opened only for a discount when purchasing furniture that you have since paid off.

If, however, the account was closed by the creditor, then there is the possibility of issues with the borrower. Accounts closed by creditors could indicate red flags to potential new lenders.

Certain situations would indicate otherwise, though, such as a mortgage or auto loan being paid off. The payment history on the account will reveal the situation to potential lenders, and you should confirm that the story it tells is accurate.

Second: When a creditor considers lending money, they consider several things. These will include at least: your income, any alimony you receive, how much money you owe, how long your loans are scheduled for, your payment history on existing accounts, how long you have had those accounts, your credit utilization ratio, as well as how much potential debt you can incur immediately.

Added together, this information reveals the level of credit risk you pose as a client.

Example:

You have a mortgage, equity line, two major credit cards (MJ CC-1 and 2), a department store credit card (DS CC), and a hardware store credit card (HS CC), *(see example (c) at chapter end for table view)*.

Your mortgage is considered positive debt because you are establishing equity and your home is an asset. All others are negative debt, which is the focus of this particular example.

Your equity line is for $50,000, MJ CC-1 has a credit line of $15,000, MJ CC-2 provides a line of $10,000, DS CC a line of $5,000, and HS CC a credit line of $10,000.

When a lender looks at this and adds up all of these credit lines, they see a potential immediate debt possibility of $90,000 on top of the existing mortgage. Because these accounts are already open and immediately accessible to you, you have access to that money.

At any moment, you could go on a shopping spree and rack up $90,000 worth of negative debt!

On another note that must be taken into consideration, the lender could also consider all of this as part of your credit utilization ratio, discussed later with credit scores in chapter 11.

Using this example, we will now focus only on the *concept of negative debt and how to lower it.*

> **This is for example only.**
> **As every situation is different, this approach will pertain to you only if it will benefit you financially, help improve your credit score and credit utilization ratio.**

Okay, back to the example.

What if the HS CC hasn't been used since you finished remodeling your home eight years ago? And MJ CC-2 is only in case of emergencies, and regularly maintains a zero balance?

If that is the case, then it could be in your best interest to close one or both of these accounts, unless they prove helpful to your credit utilization ratio, which is vital to your overall credit score.

And, if you thought you had already closed them, now is the time to follow up with the written request and notification to the credit bureaus.

As for the MJ CC-1 and DS CC cards, do you really need credit lines of $15,000 and $5,000? If you need to repair your credit, then probably not.

However, you won't want to close both of them, and the DS CC might prove useful for holiday shopping and coupons that are offered only to card holders.

In this situation, consider contacting the creditors and requesting a credit line reduction.

In truth, an MJ CC-1 credit line of $10,000 and a DS CC line of $1,000 will help you survive the holidays and otherwise (hopefully), be more credit than you need on a regular basis.

If you only made these four changes, (closing the HS CC and MJ CC-2 lines and lowering the DS CC and MJ CC-1 lines), your available debt would be reduced by $29,000 to $61,000. Although this is still a large number, it has already reduced your debt potential considerably, by a whopping 32.22%!

Note that these changes could only be made if your current balance on the account in question reflected an amount lower than your new credit line request.

If the balances are currently too high to lower the line (or you have a balance and cannot close them), then keep this strategy in mind for whenever your balances provide the opportunity to strike.

Although you do need to exercise caution when closing accounts, in general, if you don't need it and if it is not beneficial to your credit utilization ratio while your goal is to fix your credit, then get rid of it.

Always consider all pertinent details prior to closing any account.

The more you do voluntarily to show financial responsibility, the more appealing you appear on paper to potential lenders.

Example (c): Hypothetical Accounts Status*

Account Creditor	Credit Line	Interest Rate
DS CC	$5,000	25%
Home Equity	$50,000	8%
HS CC	$10,000	20%
MJ CC-1	$15,000	18%
MJ CC-2	$10,000	15%
Potential Debt	**$90,000**	
After Suggested Strategy		
DS CC	$1,000	25%
Home Equity	$50,000	8%
HS CC	*Possibly Closed*	n/a
MJ CC-1	$10,000	18%
MJ CC-2	*Possibly Closed*	n/a
New Potential Debt	**$61,000**	

For this example, only the account credit lines are adjusted (or possibly closed, unless beneficial to your credit utilization ratio). Of course, if interest rates were adjusted, then those should also be reflected here.

The purpose of this example is merely to indicate the potential debt possibilities before and after analyzing your accounts.

SUMMARY:
REPORTED ACCOUNTS

Take the time to implement these tips for any reported accounts to build better credit as quickly as possible:

» Review all accounts and confirm they are yours

» Carefully review your situation and construct a strategy beneficial to your credit score and credit utilization ratio *prior to taking any action* with any line of credit

» Close open accounts that you do not use or need (this should be done in writing), using caution to not close too many too soon or to close any that help your credit utilization ratio

» Request lower credit lines on any open accounts that you can realistically cut back unless vital to your credit utilization ratio

Chapter 4

BUDGETING

*W**hy Should I Budget?*

Admittedly, budgeting is never on the fun-things-to-do list. However, it is crucial to the success of fixing your credit and establishing future financial stability.

Understanding your financial obligations is necessary. How much money is coming in and how much is going out (and where it is going), are all revealed when a budget is created. Having this information available to review and examine every week can influence your purchasing decisions.

Now is the time to grasp the concept of budgeting and begin applying it daily to repair your credit as quickly and painlessly as possible.

Gather your expense/income sheet that you put together. This will be a useful tool and your new best friend as you work on this project and complete step three of the process.

Review all expenses listed and compare them to your credit report. If you notice any accounts that have been open for at least six months on your expense sheet but not the credit report, then the odds are strong those creditors do not report to the agencies.

At the same time, compare the reported accounts to your expense sheet to confirm the information being reported matches your records.

On a side note, an auto loan reported as $350 per month but in reality is $300 per month can throw off your debt-to-income ratio and needs to be corrected as quickly as possible.

This issue must be addressed with the creditor who is required to report the correct information to the credit agencies. It will be up to you to follow up and confirm the correction takes place, so make sure you check back.

*N*eeds Vs. Wants

Once you have verified your current expenses against the credit report, you can proceed with setting up your budget.

Begin by looking at your shopping and spending habits. When you look over your accounts, in particular your credit card statements, ask yourself if what you are purchasing are *NEEDS* or *WANTS*.

Also consider this when grocery shopping (never go when hungry), entertainment expenses and other miscellaneous and often wasteful purchases.

Again, you must be honest with yourself on this, as well as all other aspects of this project, if you want to succeed as quickly as possible. *This cannot be stressed enough!*

Now review what you owe each month for each account. Look at the minimum amount due to maintain steady, timely payments. It is imperative when repairing your credit to create and maintain consistency with reported payments.

This is not to say that unreported accounts can be ignored or pushed to the back burner. For example, electric companies seldom report, but can you afford to have your power shut off? Me neither.

Therefore, know that all accounts are equally important, some simply take priority when figuring out the amounts to be paid until the full amount can be handled without going hungry.

With that said, there are a few things to consider when analyzing how much to pay which creditor.

First, is interest being charged? If so, how much? Make a note next to each account if interest is accruing and at what percentage.

Also note whether or not there is a penalty for paying down a balance before the loan comes due. If so, then such an account should not receive more than the payment required in order to prevent additional penalties.

Which Accounts Require Top Priority?

Now that you know which account balances are accruing interest and at which rate, you can determine which ones become top priority.

Top priority, again, does not mean ignoring other debt. It simply means those accounts require more attention first.

What kind of attention? Great question!

Start with the basics. If you have two major credit cards with a balance, one with a 22% interest and one with a 15% interest, then you can see the first one will cost you more whenever you carry a balance.

Assuming neither card is maxed, take the one with the higher interest rate out of your wallet. Lock it up in a safe, but out of sight place.

Do not add to this card's balance (online or off), but rather focus on paying it off. Only when necessary, use the other credit card with the lower rate for new purchases.

Accounts with the highest interest rate will cost the most every month. These are the accounts you want to pay above the minimum due as frequently as possible.

At the beginning, this might sound daunting. But as you adjust your spending habits and money allocation, you will see it start to work.

Recent government changes now require all credit card statements show not only the balance due, but also the amount you will pay if only the minimum is paid and how long it will take. There are a couple of other payment structure/time frames included on each statement, *(see example (d) in this chapter)*.

Take a moment to review your statement and familiarize yourself with how much your current debt could possibly cost you.

Keep those larger numbers in mind every time you go to pull out a credit card for a frivolous purchase. *Can you, in truth, really afford what it will eventually cost you?*

If you don't really need it, do yourself a favor and leave it at the store.

For larger purchases in particular, sleep on it for a few nights and see if you can live without it. You might surprise yourself with how easy it is to say "No" to needless additional expenses.

Now that you have determined your top priority expenses based on level of importance (mortgage/rent), and amount of interest being charged, you can begin structuring a monthly budget plan.

Example (d): Actual Payment Information From Creditor*

PAYMENT INFORMATION
New Balance $7,851.00

| Minimum Payment Due | 158.00 |
| Payment Due Date | May 8, 2016 |

Late Payment Warning: If we do not receive your minimum payment by the date listed above, you may have to pay a late fee up to $35.00 and your purchase and balance transfer APRs for new transactions may be increased up to the Penalty APR of 18.99% variable.

Minimum Payment Warning: If you make only the minimum payment each period, you will pay more in interest and it will take you longer to pay off your balance. For example:

If you make no additional charges using this card and each month you pay...	You will pay off the balance shown on this statement in about...	And you will end up paying an estimated total of...
Only the minimum	20 years	$15,909
$261	3 years	$9,394 (Savings = $6,515)

This is actual payment information from a creditor. Notice the portion in the shaded boxes and the figures below them. If only the minimum payment is paid per month, then it will take 20 years to pay off an original balance of $7,851. If all payments are made on time, the interest charged is a whopping $8,058, making the total paid $15,909!

Note the Late Payment Warning details. If, at any time, a payment is late, then the APR could rise, in addition to fees applied for late payments.

This example should be enough to scare anyone into paying down a debt as quickly as possible, rather than relying on the simplicity of only making a minimum payment.

Just think of what you could do with an extra $8,058 in your pocket...and this is only from one credit card!

Put your mindset in gear to accomplish your goal and embrace the task at hand.

Track your spending on a daily basis for each month. Notice where the money is going and start cutting out unnecessary purchases.

Think smart before spending money.

Realize that every dime counts and consider every purchase carefully. Fine tune your spending habits and understand that even though it goes on a piece of plastic when you buy it, you will eventually have to pay for it.

If you do not have the cash to pay for it, assume you cannot afford it—until you actually can.

Dine in more frequently and enjoy the leftovers. If you must use a debit card, only use it where you will not incur fees.

Examine where you can make changes, even small ones, and apply them for greater savings and less spending.

A positive mindset to maintain while working through this phase of your financial life is to live beneath your means and spend money like you are broke.

Please do not interpret this as a negative attitude toward money. The concept is to keep you on track when you are tempted to spend.

Learn to live with less fluff and more grit.
In the end, you will be glad you did!

SUMMARY:
BUDGETING

Mastering the art of budgeting your finances will build a stronger financial future. Be sure to include these tips:

» Create a tracker or list of all expenses: monthly, semi-annual and annual

» Include all income (after taxes)

» Track all purchases: cash, credit or otherwise

» Continuously review where money is going and cut back wherever possible

» Be honest with yourself about your money: where it is going and is it necessary

» Live "broke" to fine tune spending habits

Chapter 5

CONTACTING CREDITORS

Contacting Creditors: Not So Scary

The concept of contacting creditors might sound scary at first. However, this approach to working out your credit issues gets a gold star for a few very good reasons.

To begin with, if you reach out to creditors to discuss your account, they will understand your intentions are to make good on your debt. Whether or not you have fallen behind by the time you contact them is not the point, the point is to do it.

If you have not fallen behind yet but can see things are getting tight and you will be late, now is the time to give them a call. If you do, take detailed notes, including the date and time of the call and to whom you spoke.

Always confirm the details of your account with a creditor. Confirm the amount of your debt, the payment structure and minimum due. If it is a loan, also confirm how long it is for, the number of remaining months and the interest rate, if applicable.

How To Reduce Interest

If the account is one that charges interest, ask them if they can lower the rate. Often, this can bring a positive response and if so, this one difference alone can save you hundreds (if not thousands) of dollars over the time it will take to pay off your debt.

Next, address the debt itself with your creditor. Ask if the amount owed can be reduced, especially if you can prove hardship. Discuss your options with them. Negotiate a monthly payment that works for you and allows you to stay on track without starving the kids.

If an arrangement is agreed upon, make sure you understand all of the details. In some cases, there could be a relief granted of a portion of the debt which would literally reduce the total amount owed.

In others, maybe the length of time for the loan is extended in order to reduce the monthly payment. Another possibility could be where the loan may be extended, but at a higher interest rate.

If the last option is the only option, try not to panic over the requirements.

Although the interest rate might be higher, at least the monthly payment obligation has been reduced to a more manageable amount.

If the account does not come with pre-pay penalties, then when your money frees up, contribute extra money per month (or however often) toward the principal directly, to bring the balance down.

> ***Whenever paying additional toward a loan, indicate with the payment that it is to be applied toward principal only. This should ultimately reduce the amount of interest paid out over the life of the loan.***

Communicating with creditors is a must when repairing your credit. Honesty and willingness will work for you in the end when you reach out and try to make good on your debt.

This approach could also save your accounts from being turned over to collection agencies, which most people try to avoid.

In general, creditors would rather work with you personally. It not only helps them to have open communication with you, but also saves them money. When a collection agency is used, there is often a fee to the creditor for collecting the debt.

If you can avoid collection agencies, you can also avoid the frustration of the endless phone calls and messages from debt collectors.

That detail alone makes this concept...priceless!

SUMMARY:
CONTACTING CREDITORS

Stepping up and contacting creditors before they come after you is key to working with them and possibly saving your accounts. Practice these suggestions:

» Call creditors *before* they call you, preferably before the account is late; note the date of the call and to whom you spoke

» Ask to reduce overall debt and/or for lower interest rates on accounts with interest

» Try to negotiate a monthly amount you *know* you can pay

» Review the details of any negotiations with the creditor and make sure you understand them fully

» Request written correspondence including the details of the arrangement

» Initiate communication whenever necessary to discuss any changes in your situation (upcoming or otherwise)

» When communicating in writing with a creditor, always keep a copy for your records and maintain a file with notes

» Honor new arrangements granted by the creditor

Chapter 6

Consolidating Debt

How Do I Consolidate Debt?

Consolidating debt can be a very effective tool to reduce the overall amount you wind up paying in the end. There are different methods to consider and the one you choose should be the one that suits your temperament best and coincides with the options available to you.

Research & Review Options

There are credit counseling companies you can talk to and enroll in their debt management program. If you like this option, confirm the company is reputable and legitimate.

Do your research and ask questions. Many of these companies apply steep fees. Before you sign on the dotted line, understand exactly what you are agreeing to, otherwise, you could wind up in worse financial straits than when you began.

Always take notes during the consultation or request the information in writing. It is extremely important to comprehend all details of any negotiation you make, including a consolidation.

A different approach that might work better for you is a personal loan.

If your credit can support it and a reasonable interest rate is available, this method could be your golden ticket.

If you own your own home and do not have a home equity loan or line of credit, this option might be perfect. Note that in most cases of either the home equity line or loan, closing costs will be assessed, therefore increasing costs.

Again, before agreeing to any arrangement, know the details and confirm your financial obligations. You need to ensure the arrangement selected makes sense and will help you create a better financial situation.

Low Interest Rate Balance Transfer

Another way to consolidate that is worthy of going into detail and might be within your reach, is a low (or zero) interest rate balance transfer.

This concept can save you money if you honor each and every one of your payments and watch the deadlines carefully for the end of the introductory period.

It is important to understand that if you are late with any payments, even just one, you are likely to have to pay a much higher interest rate on the *entire* amount you transferred, even if it is your last payment.

When reviewing an offer for a balance transfer, read the fine print. Commit the part about late payments and the higher interest rate to memory and force yourself to *never* let a payment slide.

Otherwise, it can cost you dearly.

Example:

Using this method to consolidate debt, let's say you have the same situation as before. You have an equity line of $50,000, MJ CC-1 with an available line of $15,000, MJ CC-2 with a line of $10,000, DS CC with a credit line of $5,000 and an HS CC credit line of $10,000.

For this example, *(see example (e) at chapter end for table view)*, you have balances on most accounts and have not yet requested to lower any credit lines.

At the same time, the DS CC balance is $4,000 at a rate of 25%, the HS CC balance is $3,000 at an interest rate of 20% and your current MJ CC-1 balance is $8,000 with an interest rate of 18%, while your MJ CC-2, having an interest rate of 15%, is vacant.

In addition, you have the home equity line with a balance of $30,000 at a fixed interest rate of only 8%.

Goal:

Now, let's analyze these accounts collectively. The goal is to see where money can be moved to in order to start saving money while paying down the debt.

Beginning with the credit cards, you can see there is a little wiggle room on the MJ CC-1 and the interest rate is already lower than either of the other two cards that have a balance.

Better yet, MJ CC-2 has a zero balance and provides a lower interest rate than all other credit cards. As we are discussing consolidation, how to use this card is now where our focus moves to.

Creditors often send balance transfer opportunities to their clients to entice them to use their line of credit. If you have received an offer, check out the details. If not, you can ask the creditor if you qualify for an opportunity.

Always begin with the account providing the lowest interest rate on purchases and balance transfers. In this case, inquire if there is an opportunity for a balance transfer on MJ CC-2, because it has the lowest current balance of zero.

*H*ow Does A Balance Transfer Work?

If you have the green light to participate in a transfer, these are the things you need to keep in mind: length of time for transfer offer, how much will it cost you and how much can you transfer while staying within your credit line (this total must include the balance transfer fee).

When transferring to a credit card, it is best to transfer to one that has a zero balance (or as close to it as possible). This is because some credit companies will apply payments to the portion of debt that has the lowest interest rate accruing first. *Always confirm this detail with your credit card companies.*

> *Note if your credit company practices this method of payment application. If so, then beware that any existing debt at a higher interest rate will continue accruing interest at that rate while you pay down the debt with the lower interest rate first.*

You're ready to do a transfer, and you know there is a total of $7,000 credit available on MJ CC-1 because it carries a balance. Based on the possibility mentioned about debt with a higher interest rate being paid *after* the debt with the lower interest rate, this card should not be the first option for a transfer.

Additionally, you should not max out this card. You need room for purchases, and in truth, it is best if you can avoid hitting your maximum limit on any card.

Because MJ CC-2 is open without a balance, this would be the ideal card to move money to, especially if a low or zero percent interest rate is available for balance transfers.

With a credit line of $10,000 available on MJ CC-2, you will be able to transfer at least $9,000 of other debt. If you transfer the combined balances of $7,000 from the DS CC and HS CC lines, you would clear those two accounts completely.

If you want to use the additional $2,000 available on the transfer request, then you can clear a tad bit off of MJ CC-1.

Transferring $2,000 from MJ CC-1 to MJ CC-2 at 0% interest would result in saving the accruing interest rate of 18% on that $2,000 for the duration of the transfer's offer.

W*hat Are My Savings?*

Most balance transfer offers are for twelve, fifteen or eighteen months. The minimum monthly payment is generally around ten percent of the new balance (always confirm the details of any transfer or transaction).

If you took advantage of a twelve month offer at 0% interest and made the transfers as described above, then your savings would be at least:

» MJ CC-1: $2,000 x .18 (18%) = $360
» DS CC: $4,000 x .25 (25%) = $1,000
» HS CC: $3,000 x .20 (20%) = $600

This example provides for a total savings the first year of $1,960!

Note: This example is based only on the $2,000 taken from MJ CC-1 for twelve months. It does not include the rest of MJ CC-1's account balance and the fact that the entire balance of $8,000, plus compounding monthly interest, always increases the total. Taking that into consideration, you will notice even greater savings!

In addition, if your transfer was for eighteen months, the interest saved on the $2,000 taken from MJ CC-1 would be $540.

B*alance Transfer Fee*

If the balance transfer fee required for the offer was 3% of the total balance, and you transfer a total of $9,000, then the fee would be $270. This is figured simply by taking the total amount being transferred and multiplying it by the fee ($9,000 x .03 = $270), bringing the new balance on MJ CC-2 up to $9,270.

Taking the estimated savings for only twelve months from the three accounts ($360 + $1,000 + $600 = $1,960) and subtracting the fee of $270, you will still see a savings that first year of at least $1,690!

So far, you have cleared two accounts that you can either close or re-duce the credit line to improve your credit rating (if either strategy are in your best interest, depending on your credit utilization ratio).

Now, let's look at the remaining balance of $6,000 on MJ CC-1.

If you are either unable to make payments and/or can only make the minimums, then you will want to move this if possible.

Per our example, if your home equity line is current, that would be the best place to move it to. It has a fixed interest rate of only 8% and has room to receive the debt.

Moving $6,000 from MJ CC-1's 18% interest for twelve months, ($6,000 x .18 = $1,080) to the home equity line's 8% interest for twelve months, ($6,000 x .08 = $480), will save you $600, ($1080 - $480 = $600) the first year, providing you maintain current payments on your equity line.

After all of this, if you maintain current payments, your first twelve months of savings should be around $2,290!

Now, with MJ CC-1 cleared up, you can reduce the credit line if you desire. Most importantly, though, you must make it a *top priority* to only charge what you can afford to pay monthly, if you use the credit card at all.

This approach should, hopefully, allow you to pay the balance on MJ CC-1 in full every month. This method of paying eliminates interest charges and also immediately assists in improving your credit by showing prompt, complete payments.

Via this example consolidation, you now have only three payments between the above mentioned creditors. Your MJ CC-1 (for any monthly purchases), the home equity line at 8% interest, and MJ CC-2 at 0% interest for the duration of the balance transfer offer.

This set up should be more manageable and far less overwhelming.

*H*ow Do I Protect Myself If Using A Balance Transfer?

To protect yourself, you must stay timely on all payments. Missing even one payment is not an option. Take precaution and set reminders in calendars for a month *before* your balance transfer introductory rate expires.

In addition, *do not use MJ CC-2 for anything* until the entire balance is paid in full.

> ### *IMPORTANT:*
> *It is imperative to either pay off the entire amount owed before the balance transfer expires or move the remaining balance to another account with a low rate.*
>
> *If you do not, you will be charged full interest on the entire balance transferred from the original date of transfer.*

In other words, to use the balance transfer approach for consolidation purposes, you must exercise caution and strict discipline. If you do not, you could experience additional expenses that could adversely impact your progress and overall goal.

*W*hich Option(s) Apply To Me?

Deciding which option is best suited to your needs is something only you can determine. Each person must consider their own specific situation, dedication to the task, temperament and tolerance for payment structure in order to select the best option for them.

But what if you don't have a credit card to transfer a balance to? Or an equity line available to borrow from? What if your credit cards are charged to the hilt and you don't have any borrowing options available at reasonable interest rates?

Admittedly, this is a tougher situation to maneuver through, but do not get discouraged. If you feel you must consolidate and there are no other options, you can always use a professional service. Again, confirm all details and understand how much it will cost if you go this route and always research any company before hiring them.

And, although you could ask to borrow money from friends or family to pay off your credit cards, there could be other consequences. Yes, you might save money on some interest, but this option can certainly bring its own set of challenges. On that note, you might wish to reconsider.

If you decide to go it on your own, then budgeting and communication with creditors will be even more important players in your process.

This is when your payment negotiation and paying technique savvy will truly get their workout.

Example (e): Hypothetical Accounts Consolidation Per Above Strategy*

Current Account Balances & Status			
Account or Creditor	**Credit Line**	**Balance / Interest**	**Annual Interest**
DS CC	$5,000	$4,000 / 25%	$1,000
Home Equity	$50,000	$30,000 / 8%	$2,400
HS CC	$10,000	$3,000 / 20%	$600
MJ CC-1	$15,000	$8,000 / 18%	$1,440
MJ CC-2	$10,000	$0 / 15%	$0
Totals	**$90,000**	**$45,000**	**$5,440**
Consolidated Account Balances & Status			
DS CC	$1,000	$0 / 25%	$0
Home Equity	$50,000	$36,000 / 8%	$2,880
HS CC	*Closed*	n/a	n/a
MJ CC-1	$10,000	Varies / 18%	*If paid*, $0
MJ CC-2**	$10,000	$9,270 / 0%	$0
Totals	**$71,000**	**$45,270**	**$2,880**
Total Interest Savings For This 12 Month Period			**$2,560**

Entire table figured per only one twelve month period with interest rates based on balance as indicated and not reflecting payments credited.

DS CC and MJ CC-1 credit limits reduced; HS CC closed by consumer request. MJ CC-1 "if paid" = balance paid in full monthly by due date.

**The MJ CC-2's balance transfer introductory 0% interest rate is used but only lasts as long as the transfer offer indicates.*

Note that after the initial twelve months, if not paid off or moved to another account, the rate will increase, generally to the full interest rate (currently, per example, 15%) and retro back to the beginning of the transfer.

IMPORTANT: Have a plan in place prior to the introductory rate's expiration of where to move the balance to if not able to pay off in time!

SUMMARY: CONSOLIDATING DEBT

Consolidating debt can be very beneficial. Review these tips when considering your options:

» Review all accounts, credit lines, balances and interest rates/fees

» Consider balance transfer offers to a lower interest rate opportunity

» Ensure credit line available will support required transfer fee(s) for balance transfers

» Whether consolidating on your own or using a service, always review and understand all details (length of time, interest rate, fees, grace periods, late payment penalties, etc.)

» Do the math. Make sure your next move is in the right direction and suits your needs

» When nearing an offer's end date, be prepared to either pay the balance off entirely or move the money to another, low interest account

» Practice caution and discipline, especially with balance transfers

Chapter 7

PAYMENT PLANS

Setting Up A Structured Payment Plan

Now that you know the status of each account, it is time to set up a structured payment plan if one is not already in place. Before rushing to call anyone about a plan, take a moment to do a few things first.

Review the budget sheet you created along with your current credit report. Take note of which creditors are reporting to the agencies (the account and payment history will be posted on your report), and which ones are not, and mark them accordingly on your budget sheet.

To start off on the right foot, make sure you set up the best situation possible for each account. Contact your creditors directly and discuss setting up a payment plan for every applicable account.

Even if an account has already been sent to a collection agency, begin by contacting the original creditor.

If they are willing to work with you, it could save both of you money. In addition, they have the power to report your payments to the credit agencies, which will help rebuild your credit.

Remember, consistent, timely payments pave the way for a higher credit score and overall improved credit rating.

*T*alking With Creditors

It is best to be prepared prior to placing the call. Figure out how much you can pay while working on your budget. This will allow you to have a solid picture of what you can afford while attempting a negotiation.

When talking with creditors, if you want to approach them about settling for a lower balance due, then ask them if they can work with you on a percentage of the debt and waive the rest. In some cases, this strategy is a stronger possibility than others, such as medical bills, although there are no guarantees.

Regardless of which creditor you speak to, always do your best to negotiate payments to an amount you know you can meet on a regular basis.

As previously mentioned, be aware that negotiating a lower minimum payment might cost you more in interest. Try not to worry about this detail yet. This should not be where your focus is right now.

When getting started, the most important thing will be to keep your promise and make the required payments on time.

In other words, avoid setting yourself up for failure.

Hopefully, over time, you will be able to pay more than the monthly minimum and will therefore be able to clear the debt prior to paying all of the interest.

If you do decide to pay above the minimum, always indicate on the payment stub that the additional amount is to go to principal only (this option is not generally applicable on credit cards).

*N*egotiating & Interest Rates

When negotiating with smaller companies or older debt accounts that charge interest, ask if it is possible to waive future interest charges.

Some companies would rather sacrifice the interest (after you commit to a definite payment plan), in lieu of not being paid or having to hire a collection agency to track down monies owed.

Once the payment structure is agreed upon, request the details in writing. In addition, always keep your own notes with the name of the person you spoke to and the date of your call.

Organize Account Details

Start a file for each account and keep all notes about conversations, negotiations and payments organized for quick reference.

For visual reminders, create a list or spreadsheet with the accounts and updated payment information. Post it where you can refer to it easily and often.

Maximize your opportunities and stick to the plan, and you will watch your debt disappear!

SUMMARY:
PAYMENT PLANS

Structured payment plans can help keep you on track. Keep these things in mind as you set them up:

» Review budget sheet details and figure out how much money can realistically be allotted to each account

» Attempt to negotiate payment amounts within your reach to maintain regular, timely payments

» Always contact a creditor if you know you will be late with a payment *before* you are late

» Maintain accurate records about each conversation or communication with creditors for each account

» Whenever possible, work directly with the creditor rather than a collection agency

» Create a list or spreadsheet with updated account payment requirements for quick reference

Chapter 8

Making Payments

Strategies For Timely Payments

The importance of making timely payments cannot be overstated. It is the backbone to making this process work and ties in heavily to how you communicate with creditors, both those you currently owe as well as those who consider lending to you in the future.

Regardless of whether or not you were able to consolidate debt into fewer payments such as previously illustrated, you will need to master the art of making payments.

Now that you have negotiated balances and interest rates, set up structured payment plans and possibly consolidated accounts, it is time to start paying as promised.

The general strategy (and first priority), is to pay all of your creditors as agreed upon during negotiation. However, there are additional tactics to consider, which might be useful at some point and time.

Note that most creditors have agreed to set up your plan based on a minimum amount due on regular intervals. Each account will be different, but as you refer to your notes, highlight those that charge interest on the outstanding balance.

Also note which one has the highest interest rate, next highest and so on. In addition, track the accounts that report your payments to the credit agencies.

Obviously, there are times when circumstances change that can alter your financial situation. Therefore, keep these details in mind because you might find yourself needing to adjust how you pay which creditor.

It is during one such time when you might need to temporarily adjust your plan. This concept is not to be used unnecessarily, nor is it to be abused.

Remember, the overall goal is to rebuild your credit and increase your credit rating.

Abusing any suggestion that could help save you in a time of emergency could ultimately undo any good you have accomplished.

Example:

L et's use the previous hypothetical account situation as shown in example (e) (page 37), *without* any consolidation, but with a payment plan in place for both the HS CC and the DS CC, instead.

After negotiations, your hypothetical monthly obligations are 10% of your balance to the HS CC, and $100 a month to the DS CC until paid. The hardware store refused to waive future interest fees, but the department store agreed, while having frozen your account until the outstanding balance is paid in full.

The remaining two accounts, MJ CC-1 and the home equity line, charge the minimum due each month (plus accruing interest on the outstanding balance).

Therefore, you now have three accounts charging interest: the home equity line at 8%, HS CC at 20%, and MJ CC-1 at 18%.

In addition, out of all four of the accounts, the only one that does not report to the credit agency is the HS CC *(for this example only; always confirm reporting entities via your credit report)*.

After a few months of making payments as agreed, there is a family emergency to which you must allocate money that would otherwise go toward a payment. You realize you will not be able to make the minimum payments to all of your accounts and need to improvise.

It is time to get creative and consider your options.

*C*reating Solutions In Payment Emergency

Upon review of your accounts, you know that the HS CC does not report your payment activity, but they are still charging interest. Yet, the DS CC, who has agreed to waive interest, does report.

Revisit your notes pertaining to the negotiations. When you discussed your payment plan with the DS CC, did they indicate if you paid less than your minimum or missed a payment, that they would charge full interest on the original balance and continue charging interest going forward?

If there is not a penalty for paying less than the agreed amount, then this is your window.

Again, you would not want to make this a habit. However, in this situation you could, for a month or two, contemplate paying a portion of your payment to the DS CC and use the remainder as a partial payment to the HS CC.

Although this approach will not save you entirely, it will show good faith in attempt to pay your debt and the creditor will see you are not ignoring your responsibility.

Another strategy would be to pay the highest interest accounts first.

Note that any missed payments on reporting accounts will be acknowledged in your credit file, along with how many days late the payment was (30, 60, 90, etc.), and work against you.

Whereas a timely payment of less than the required minimum should also be noted on a reporting account, it will still indicate payments are being made on time.

For optimum results in any situation, it is in your best interest to contact the creditor and advise them of the issue at hand.

> *Always know and understand the repercussions for missing payments or paying less than agreed. Pay strict attention to your statements and communicate with the creditor before making your own changes to a structured payment plan.*

*S*eize Opportunities

In the event you are able to pay the minimums owed and also add to a payment, then this is a grand opportunity to seize.

Whenever you can afford to pay additional on an account, choose the one with the highest interest rate first. Paying down the balance owed should decrease the amount of interest being charged the following cycle.

If you are paying additional monies on a loan, then it is important to indicate that the additional amount is to be applied to the principal only.

Whenever you make a payment to any account, whether online, via check, transfer, money order or in person, make sure you receive a receipt or other written proof of payment with your account number on it. For online payments, request an email confirmation or take a screen shot of the completed transaction.

Keep a file of all correspondence and payments, noting which method of payment was used and when it was submitted.

SUMMARY:
MAKING PAYMENTS

How you make your payments will play a huge part in how quickly you repair your credit. Stay on track with these tips:

» Make payments on time

» Make payments of some kind to all accounts every month (or as billed)

» In case of emergencies, choose carefully how to allocate your funds, possibly considering interest rates and reporting status of accounts

» Know all details about your accounts and contact any creditors of unforeseen extenuating circumstances before making changes to how you pay them

» Pay down principal balances as soon and as quickly as possible (without jeopardizing other accounts)

» Keep detailed records of all payments; indicate any portions that are to be applied to principal balance

Chapter 9

COLLECTION AGENCIES

*K*now Your Rights

The last place you, and your creditor, want your account to wind up is with a collection agency.

If, however, your account has landed there and you have not yet contacted the creditor to work things out, it is very likely you will be (or have already been) contacted by a debt collector.

The calls and letters can be very intimidating; they are designed to be scary in order to get debtors to pay. However, this does not give the collector the right to harass you. *In fact, it is illegal to do so according to the Fair Debt Collection Practices Act.*

Just because you owe money, that does not make you a criminal. You do have rights. You need to be aware of what they are and what you do or do not have to put up with as you strive to pay off your debts.

When a collector calls you, your best bet is to have the conversation and confront the issue directly. Find out what you can about what they claim to know about you and the alleged debt.

First: Take notes of every detail from the conversation.

Ask their name and confirm the correct spelling, if necessary. Note the time and date of the call and the name of the collection agency they are calling from, their address and phone number.

Next: Ask for the name of the creditor whom they represent and how much the debt is. Inquire how you can dispute or verify it, in case you need to. Take detailed notes and confirm you understand the process described.

Note that you are merely asking questions at this time and not neces-sarily acknowledging whether or not the debt is yours.

The first step is to gather the information. When you have everything from them, then you can proceed with whichever piece of the puzzle fits next.

If the collector does not provide the information on the phone, request all details in writing.

You have the right to withhold from acknowledging you owe the mon-ey, as well as making arrangements for payments, until after you have the information in writing and have confirmed its accuracy. You should also cross reference this information with your current credit report, to verify whether or not it is there.

*H*ow To Resolve The Debt

If you know the debt is yours and the amount is accurate, then proceed with setting up a payment plan when you receive the information.

You can contact the collection agency or attempt to work with the cred-itor directly, which is generally preferred. However, please note that not all creditors will work with debtors once an account has been turned over to collections.

On the other hand, what if the debt is several years old?

In this case, research your state's statute of limitations for filing a lawsuit to collect the debt. A consultation with an attorney might be a reasonable choice for proper interpretation of the applicable laws in your area and to determine what is the best course of action for you.

What If The Debt Is Not Mine?

In addition, if you are not certain the debt is yours, then write the collection agency and request the name and address of the original creditor (if different from the current creditor). In your letter, request the amount owed and for proof the debt is yours.

If the debt is *definitely* not yours, then write the debt collector and inform them you do not owe the money in question and you do not want to be contacted about it again.

Always make and keep copies of all communication with creditors and collectors.

SUMMARY:
COLLECTION AGENCIES

Collection agencies are hired to collect debt. Although this does not make them your friend, they do not have to become your enemy. The following includes a list of things a debt collector is *not* allowed to do according to the Fair Debt Collection Practices Act:

» Call without identifying themselves

» Make repeated phone calls intended to annoy, abuse or harass you or whomever answers the phone

» Make threats of violence or harm

» Use abusive or profane language

» Publish names of people who refuse to pay their debts (this does not include reporting information to a credit company)

» If you believe you are being harassed by a debt collector, you can submit a complaint to the Consumer Financial Protection Bureau

» In addition, beware of possible scams via phone, text, email, etc., impersonating debt collectors; always exercise caution and do not volunteer personal information

Chapter 10

APPLYING FOR NEW CREDIT

Should I Apply For New Credit?

While you are rebuilding you credit, it will be in your best interest to resist applying for more credit.

The more consistent your payments become and the lower your overall debt, the more likely you will be presented with offers to either increase your credit line or apply for a new one.

Although an increase in your credit line can be beneficial to your credit utilization ratio, at this point in the process it could also be tempting to increase more debt. Because you are still mastering the art of making payments to get out of debt, any increases could backfire unless you are truly disciplined.

As for new credit cards, you should not need another department store or gas station credit card. Unless you are purchasing a prepaid credit card, then do not do it. In addition, temporarily refrain from applying for new loans.

It is important to remember the higher your debt-to-income ratio, the lower your credit score can be unless your credit utilization ratio indicates otherwise.

Goal:

Because your goal is to rebuild your credit and increase your score, applying for new credit of any kind should be put on hold until you have solid financial discipline.

When your credit is restored, a whole new world of options can, and will, eventually present themselves.

After you have successfully rebuilt your credit, you will be eligible for lower interest rates on loans you apply for and obtain. You will probably notice your minimum payments will also be more feasible because you have proven to be both willing and capable of making your payments as promised.

Prescreened & Preapproved Offers

As you prove your credit worthiness, it is likely you will start receiving prescreened credit offers. These offers generally arrive via the mail or email, usually unsolicited by you.

During your review of the offers, you might discover products and options well suited to you and your financial goals.

It could be through one of these opportunities that you eventually obtain a credit card offering updated technology and reward programs. An added bonus could also be a more reasonable rate.

These prescreened offers, or preapproved applications, are offered to individuals whose paying habits meet certain criteria by the creditors. And, even though the creditor has received your information as a borrower who meets their specifications, their method of discovery (a soft inquiry, or soft pull), does not adversely affect your credit score.

Many times the products being offered are not available to the general public. Although you might not want them in your mailbox, you might find them educational as to other options now available to you.

Additionally, it is important to note that these prescreened offers are not a guarantee you will receive a line of credit. Should you respond to the offer, a full credit check (hard inquiry, or hard pull), will be conducted to confirm your details and evaluate how much, if any, credit will be extended to you.

New credit lines may help boost your credit utilization ratio and will certainly provide more credit for you to use. However, until your credit score can absorb the ping from the hard inquiry and is sound enough to provide a positive response from creditors, it may be wise to wait to apply.

Overall, there are many positives to resisting the temptation to take on new credit cards or loans until you have made it through the bulk of the process.

Your determination to raise your credit score and improve your financial standing will serve you far into your future. If you can hold out until the process is complete, you will get there sooner.

SUMMARY:
APPLYING FOR NEW CREDIT

Applying for new credit is appealing, especially when you are used to being denied. Keep these thoughts in mind until the timing is best for your situation:

» Resist applying for new loans and credit cards, even if a discount for initial purchase is promised

» Applications for new credit will ping your credit (hard inquiry), and could potentially negatively affect your credit score

» Prescreened (preapproved) offers that are sent to you but not responded to, do not lower your credit score

» Prescreened offers are not a guarantee you will be approved for a line of credit

» New credit lines *may* potentially boost your credit utilization ratio, but not all applications for new credit will be approved

» Automatic credit line increases on existing accounts are positive indicators and improve your credit utilization ratio

Chapter 11

CREDIT SCORE

H*ow Important Is My Credit Score?*

By now, you should understand that your credit score is vital when applying for any form of credit.

The higher your credit score, the lower your interest rates, higher your credit lines (if applicable to your income), and the better your chances of being approved.

In general, credit scores range from 300–850 and the lower the score, the harder it is to borrow money. Companies use different ranges and different methods of determining the score, making it difficult to pinpoint your exact number.

You might be surprised to learn that you could have more than one credit score. This is because lenders use different scores for different products. Additionally, there are several different formulas for determining credit scores and multiple credit reporting sources.

Understanding this, could explain why you might qualify for various interest rates for the same loan or product when applying to several companies. However, the possibility of the lower rate is a solid argument as to why you should want to shop around.

Credit scores are generally based on the information found on your credit reports, which is why it is important to review them for accuracy. Credit scores are not provided on credit reports and if requested, might require a fee, yet some creditors will provide the score for free.

> *The primary credit reporting companies are Equifax®, Experian® and TransUnion®. You can request your credit report online at annualcreditreport.com.*

*V*ariables & Credit Utilization Ratio

There are several variables that can, and will, affect your credit score.

Here are the most common variables, (list not all-inclusive): how many and which types of credit accounts you have, how long you have had those accounts, how close you are to your credit limit per account, payment timeliness, number of credit inquiries, and your credit utilization ratio (or credit utilization rate, and here, CUR).

Credit utilization ratio pertains to how much credit you currently have available via your open revolving credit lines and how much you currently owe. This is applied to accounts individually as well as collectively.

Your CUR is determined by taking the existing balance total divided by your credit limit (whether on only one card or between all lines of credit) and should be less than 10%, but absolutely no more than 30%.

Let's refer to the illustration from example (e) (page 37), prior to consolidation. Taking the existing balance total of all revolving accounts and dividing by the credit limit, the credit utilization ratio is 50%.

This percentage is arrived at by taking the total current outstanding *debt* of $45,000 and dividing it by the *total available credit* of $90,000 (45,000 ÷ 90,000 = .50).

If we refer to the same example and use the amounts *after* consolidating, the new outstanding debt is $45,270, while the new overall credit available is $71,000. Once again, we divide the debt by the total available credit and find the new credit utilization ratio is 64% (45,270 ÷ 71,000 = .637).

As you can see, given this example, neither option will arrive at a favorable CUR of 30% or less. However, because everyone's CUR is different and based on their specific totals, you will have to determine which course of action is best for you.

C*losing An Account*

When you decide to close an account, confirm you are not jeopardizing a different account by using all of the credit available on the open one. And again, consider the impact on your credit utilization ratio.

Realize that having only one open credit card rather than two, can hurt your CUR instead of help it.

Having two open accounts, even if the balance is only on one card, allows for your available credit amount to be higher, which directly influences your credit utilization ratio.

Example:

A simple example would be to have two accounts, each with a $10,000 credit line. Your outstanding balance on one card is $5,000 and the other is zero.

For the one card, your CUR is 50% (5,000 ÷ 10,000 = .50), however, between the two cards (assuming these are the only two revolving accounts you have), your overall CUR is 25% (5,000 ÷ 20,000 = .25).

If you close the account with a zero balance, your CUR then becomes 50%, which is 20% higher than the suggested maximum of 30%. As you can see here, it would be best to keep both accounts open unless there is a more pressing circumstance requiring you to close an account.

Closing accounts requires scrutiny and wise use of credit.

The same applies to transferring balances. Taking advantage of this resource too frequently can hinder your credit score, especially if you repeatedly close the accounts once you transfer from them.

Think twice when making a major move with an account. Understand and respect that creditors seldom know you personally and rely heavily on the information gleaned from your report.

Understanding how to work with your accounts, which ones benefit you and how, will be instrumental in expediting the credit repair process.

However, in all circumstances, to raise your credit score or simply maintain a higher score, always pay your bills on time. In addition, do not max out your credit cards or dance near the top of your credit limit.

Longevity with a creditor speaks favorably of you and your loyalty to a company. The longer you have the account and remain in good standing, the better your score.

Remember that a potential creditor's decision can have a direct impact on situations that could be life altering, whether for or against you, such as in the attempt to purchase a new home.

SUMMARY:
CREDIT SCORE

Treat your credit score with respect and take care to use it wisely as it can become your best ally if you do. Keep your score up with these habits:

» Pay all bills consistently and on time

» Use discretion when closing accounts

» Only apply for credit when you need it

» Maintain lower balances; do not max out your credit lines

» Monitor your credit utilization ratio for highest scoring

» Limit the frequency and number of balance transfers

» Regularly review the information on your credit reports for accuracy

Chapter 12

Credit Threats

Possible Credit Threats

Everyone is exposed to possible credit threats, even those who are working to rebuild or restore their credit.

Credit threats are constantly changing and multiplying, making it impossible to include all possibilities here. However, the information provided should bring awareness to the reality of existing threats and hopefully encourage caution. Possible threats include:

» Identity theft
» Mail or online fraud and phishing
» Skimming and shimming
» Unauthorized charges

An important note to stress up front is that of familiar names and faces. Even though someone may be your spouse, relative, or best friend, that does not make them exempt from being possible threats to your credit.

If family or friends ask to borrow your card, always use caution. If you want to help them, in truth, it would be best if you made the purchase for them. This might sound silly or extreme, but if they have your information once, then they could use it without your knowledge later, possibly creating debt and causing problems for which you could be held accountable.

In such cases, should you contact your creditor to dispute the unauthorized charge(s), you might be asked to sign a sworn statement. Know that having granted them permission in the past to use your card could possibly void out the validity of your dispute, therefore making you the responsible party.

In addition, while we all want to trust our friends with our lives and first born, it is best not to trust them with our personal information. Individuals who are privy to such information could—at any time—access your credit and become an identity thief. This is an even stronger possibility if you no longer speak to each other.

I have two acquaintances who have suffered identity theft via college roommates with whom they no longer associate, so please use caution and heed this warning.

*M**ail Or Online Fraud & Phishing*

Fraud is not restricted simply to someone physically stealing your credit card. Nor is it possible to guarantee yourself foolproof protection from credit card fraud. However, you can take precautions to protect yourself—and you should.

Mail fraud is committed most commonly by mail theft. If a thief retrieves your information from your mail, then they could have access to your credit and accounts. Again, it is impossible to monitor all activities, but following a few simple rules can reduce their opportunities.

Always check all of your mail, even the junk mail. Many credit card offers arrive with all of your information preprinted, which can be an open door for a thief. Either shred or burn all pieces with personal information that you do not want.

I open all of my mail, review the pages to see which ones have any piece of personal information or account numbers and burn them. The rest go in the recycling bin.

Are you moving? Always notify the post office when you change your address. Contact all creditors and financial institutions and provide them with the new address, preferably at least twenty days before your next billing statement. This is extremely important, even if you receive all statements electronically.

Note that if you do not receive your bill, you will still be expected to pay on time. If your bill is late, contact the company to make sure they have the correct address and ensure it has been sent. Confirm your due date and the amount owed, in case the bill does not arrive.

In addition, if you pay your bills via the mail, do not leave your payments in your mailbox or an unsecured location, such as a hotel or building lobby. Always drop them off at the post office or into a secure mailbox.

Online fraud consists of thieves obtaining and/or using your credit card information online. Whether you choose to bank or shop via the Internet is irrelevant to whether or not you could become a victim of online fraud.

Do not be fooled into believing that because you do not indulge in the conveniences of online services, others will not. In fact, expect the contrary. The Internet is the preferred place to use your credit information, because identification and signatures are not required to make purchases online.

Phishing is a method of obtaining your information via emails that has become increasingly common.

The most widely used emails for this form of theft are those resembling or imitating emails from financial institutions. Note that these emails are very deceptive! They have bank logos, images, and web addresses that you would expect to see from your legitimate institution.

Opening the email does not necessarily expose you to identity theft immediately, however, responding to it probably will. If you can identify it as a fake prior to opening, then do not even open it.

If not, and you do open and respond to it, you will be directed to the scammer's website and instructed to provide your details. Such details can include your account number(s), passwords, and personal information.

DO NOT PROVIDE ANY INFORMATION!

Once they have your information, they can literally empty the account(s) and move your money into their accounts. These emails are not to be toyed with or taken lightly.

Instead, immediately close (but do not delete) the email. Then, contact the institution they are claiming to be. Give them a call or go directly to their website and inquire where and how to forward the fake email.

Next, send the phishing email to the institution and allow them to begin an investigation. Now, after having sent the email to their security division to research, mark the email as spam and finally, delete.

Currently, the best way to identify a legitimate email from your financial institution is that they will not ask for any personal information. Nor will they contact you via telephone and ask for any information, not even your credit card or account number.

> *IF you receive either phishing emails or inquisitive phone calls, do not respond with any information. If you question anything, contact the entity directly to discuss your concerns.*

Skimming & Shimming

Credit card skimming and shimming both require the use of the physical credit card. Places where your card can be skimmed or shimmed include anywhere you use the card and a dishonest employee can access it or a terminal has the skimmer or shimmer installed.

Skimming and shimming require a device that reads the account number and information from the credit card itself. Skimming reads the magnetic stripe while shimming retrieves information from the newer EMV chip cards.

Skimming devices might be easier to identify because the card reader may appear to have been tampered with, but shimming devices are much harder to detect. The primary indicator of a shimmer's presence is resistance when inserting the card into the chip reading terminal.

Use caution and be willing to refuse the credit transaction if you suspect anything unusual. In addition, refrain from using a pin number whenever possible.

Once the card has been skimmed or shimmed, the information can be used to purchase items on the phone or Internet. Your information could also be sold to create counterfeit cards.

In the case of counterfeit cards, your credit card would still work, so you would not be suspicious. However, when you check your statement, you would discover the unauthorized, fraudulent charges.

Often, by the time you see the charges in question, the counterfeit card will have been discarded for a new one. Regardless, you must report the fraudulent activity immediately and request a new card and account number from your creditor.

*U*nauthorized Charges

If your card has been lost or stolen, borrowed and not returned, misplaced, etc., contact your creditor immediately and report it as lost. Most companies have customer service lines that never close for lost or stolen cards. The sooner you act, the less opportunity exists for unauthorized charges to wind up on your account.

Any and all unauthorized charges must be reported to the creditor as soon as you discover them. It is irrelevant if the card is still in your possession or the purchases were made online, it only matters that you did not authorize the purchase(s).

The first thing to do is immediately contact the credit card company. Take notes of the phone call, including: the date, to whom you speak, the charge(s) or activity in question, action you are required to take, and the outcome of the call.

Discuss your financial responsibilities with the creditor. In many cases, you could have zero liability for the charge(s). In others, you might be responsible for up to $50 (currently, this limit is per card and set by federal law). Always inquire about the specifics for your particular card type and account.

Unless your creditor provides this service, follow the phone call with a letter to your creditor outlining the fraudulent activity. Include a copy of the portion of your statement showing the transactions, highlighting the unauthorized charge(s). Maintain a copy of your correspondence for your records.

If you have the option, set up alerts with your creditors. Most credit card companies will contact you immediately upon receipt of a suspicious charge. If you receive an alert, respond as quickly as possible to prevent further charges from occurring.

These alerts are valuable and highly recommended.

If you are the victim of identity theft, you are entitled to a free copy of your credit report, per the Fair Credit Reporting Act. In addition, you might also wish to place a fraud alert on your credit report. Discuss the option with the credit agency to decide if this route is one you would like to pursue.

If you decide to use a credit monitoring service, research the company first. Understand all fees involved and the details of the service(s) they provide.

Also, contact your state to learn of possible reporting laws that could provide you with additional rights. To find this information, begin with government agencies in your area.

Although this is a lot to absorb, I hope it brings awareness and validity to the importance of monitoring and protecting your credit.

Taking everything you have read into consideration, hopefully you will make it a habit to check your statements frequently and review your credit report thoroughly at least once a year.

SUMMARY:
CREDIT THREATS

Know that it is impossible to guarantee you will never be a victim of credit fraud, but be aware and use caution. Protect your credit with these habits:

» Do not lend your credit card or account information

» Always confirm you receive your card back from public transactions

» Monitor statement activity frequently

» Report all unauthorized charges or suspicious activity immediately to your creditor

» Do not provide personal or account information in emails or via phone calls that you do not initiate

» Be aware of your surroundings and suspicious individuals; never leave your purse or wallet unattended

» Set up alerts with credit card companies

» Use secure and trusted websites when shopping online

Conclusion

Now that you have cleaned up your credit and are on track with paying your bills, it is time for a hearty congratulation!

This process is most rewarding once completed. Throughout this experience, you should have learned (at least) how to:

» Budget your money better

» Review and understand your credit report

» Communicate openly with creditors

» Set up structured payment plans

» Refrain from unnecessary purchases that can destroy your budget and lower your credit score

» Maintain a healthy credit score

» Be aware and cautious of possible credit threats

If you choose to hire a service to help you repair your credit or eliminate debt, research them carefully.

For a quick recap, following is a list of high points covered within this book to keep you on track. Having worked so hard to repair your credit and boost your credit score, you certainly don't want to let it slip away again!

Review your accounts and rejoice in the lower balances (or no balance); always check your credit reports a few times a year.

Annual reviews from each credit reporting company should be sufficient unless you have reason to suspect fraud.

Double check each account and confirm your creditors have been posting your payments accurately. If you have closed any accounts, confirm the status is reflected on your credit file and it states the account was closed by consumer.

Use caution when consolidating debt. Confirm all details of the transaction in writing and never miss a payment.

Continue making better purchasing decisions and timely payments. Resist opening too many lines of credit.

Do not lend your credit card(s) or account information; do not disclose to phishing emails or phone solicitors.

Enjoy the flexibility and freedom you have with more credit available and a higher credit score, but do not abuse it.

Never forget how costly and challenging it can be to rebuild your credit.

And, most importantly, give yourself that much deserved pat on the back for setting a goal, working hard, and achieving it!

Wishing you all the best in your financial success,

Kendyl

ACKNOWLEDGMENT

Special thanks and sincere appreciation go to Helen and Linda.

These ladies are two important individuals who not only support me in my endeavors and truly believe in my quest to help others, but also review my writing. They provide valuable insight, comments and suggestions, for which I am grateful.

ABOUT THE AUTHOR

Kendyl Jameson writes of her experiences and what she has learned from them. She hopes by sharing with others, she can empower her readers to live their best lives.

In addition to *DIY Credit Repair: Beginners' Guide to Credit Repair*, (also available in Spanish, *DIY Reparación de Crédito: Guía del principiante para la reparación del crédito*), she has written *DIY Credit Builder: Beginners' Guide to Building Credit*.

These guides are intended to help others build, fix, and maintain a healthy credit score, while learning how to understand and manage one's finances.

Her work also includes *The Pirates of My Soul: A Transformational Voyage to Self-Empowerment*. This memoir encapsulates her relationships, wherein she shares personal observations and analysis with readers. Her story is revealing, entertaining and empowering, while touching on relatable topics.

If you like her work, please leave a review on Amazon (where all books may be purchased) and Goodreads.com.

Learn more about her books and follow Kendyl on Amazon. Visit the links below or scan the QR code to go directly to Kendyl's author page.

Facebook.com/KendylJameson
KendylJameson.com
@KendylJameson

www.ingramcontent.com/pod-product-compliance
Lightning Source LLC
Chambersburg PA
CBHW071630040426

42452CB00009B/1564